The FBI

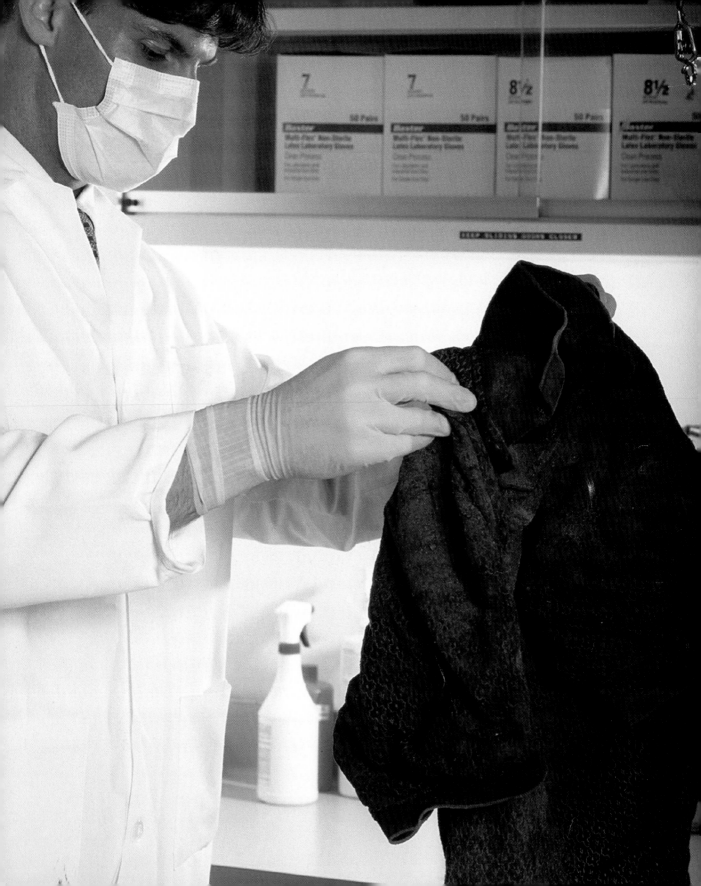

The FBI

Brendan January

Watts LIBRARY™

Franklin Watts
A Division of Scholastic Inc.
New York • Toronto • London • Auckland • Sydney
Mexico City • New Delhi • Hong Kong
Danbury, Connecticut

Note to readers: Definitions for words in **bold** can be found in the Glossary at the back of this book.

The photograph on the cover shows FBI agents arresting members of the Russian mob, Vyachelav Ivankov (front) and Leonid Abellis (back), in June 1995. The photograph opposite the title page shows an FBI pathologist examining evidence at a laboratory in Quantico, Virginia, in the 1990s.

Photographs © 2002: AP/Wide World Photos: 41 (Bob Daugherty), 51 (John Gaps III), cover (Monika Graff), 50 (David Longstreath), 47 (Joe Marquette), 38 (Suzanne Plunkett), 42 (Linda Spillers), 17, 21, 26, 28; Corbis Images: 6 (AFP), 14, 16, 18, 24, 29, 33, 34, 37 (Bettman), 2, 43 (Anna Clopet), 30 (Flip Schulke), 9; Corbis Sygma: 44; Folio, Inc./Everett C. Johnson: 8; Hulton|Archive/Getty Images: 49 (Calvin Hom/Reuters), 10, 23; National Archives at College Park: 13; The Image Works/Topham: 27.

Library of Congress Cataloging-in-Publication Data

January, Brendan, 1972-
    The FBI / Brendan January.
        p. cm. — (Watts library)
    Includes bibliographical references and index.
    Summary: An introduction to the structure and purpose of the FBI.
    ISBN 0-531-12033-3 (lib. bdg.)   0-531-16601-5 (pbk.)
    1. United States. Federal Bureau of Investigation—Juvenile literature. 2. Criminal investigation—United States—Juvenile literature. [1. United States. Federal Bureau of Investigation.] I. Title. II. Series.
HV8144.F43 J36 2002
363.25'0973—dc21   2001005728

Contents

In response to the terrorist attacks of September 11, 2001, President George W. Bush immediately ordered the Federal Bureau of Investigation to investigate the disaster and to take steps to prevent future attacks. Here, FBI workers get their IDs checked at the World Trade Center site in lower Manhattan ten days after the attacks.

Terrorism Strikes

September 11, 2001, dawned bright and clear. In New York City, thousands of workers arrived in their offices at the World Trade Center, where the Twin Towers soared 110 stories above the skyline. At about the same time, four passenger jets were taking off from airports in Boston, Newark, and Washington, D.C. On board each jet, hijackers overwhelmed the passengers and crew, seized the controls, and steered the planes toward new destinations.

The FBI is headquartered in the J. Edgar Hoover FBI Building in Washington, D.C. The entrance pictured here faces Pennsylvania Avenue.

At 8:47 A.M., the first jet streaked in low over New York City and slammed into the north tower. Fifteen minutes later, a second jet approached from the southwest and dove into the south tower. At 9:50 A.M., the south tower crumbled to the ground in an avalanche of glass, smoke, dust, and pulverized concrete. The north tower fell 28 minutes later.

Earlier that morning, in Washington, D.C., the third plane had crashed into the Pentagon, the headquarters of the U.S. military. Over Ohio, passengers on another flight made frantic cell-phone calls to report that they had been hijacked. They told relatives of their plan to resist the hijackers. Over western Pennsylvania, the fourth plane streaked downward and exploded in a field.

The hijackers, allegedly part of a terrorist organization led by Osama bin Laden, had killed nearly three thousand people. Across the country, schools and businesses were closed, planes were grounded, and people gathered together in shock and outrage.

President George W. Bush spoke to calm the nation. "Freedom itself was attacked this morning, and I assure you freedom will be defended," he said. To help defend that freedom, Bush turned to the nation's elite law-enforcement organization: the Federal Bureau of Investigation, or FBI.

The FBI Today

It was not the first time an American president had relied on the FBI. With a budget of $3.5 billion and eleven thousand

agents, the FBI is a powerful weapon against crime. Most agents report to one of fifty-six field offices scattered throughout the country, including one in Puerto Rico. Field offices vary in size from one agent in Cumberland, Maryland, to more than twelve hundred agents in New York City. FBI agents are investigators for the U.S. Department of Justice, which is directed by the attorney general of the United States.

The FBI can investigate more than 250 crimes at the same time. It catches spies, breaks down organized crime, profiles serial murderers, and tracks down drug smugglers, bombers, and art thieves. The bureau also serves as one of the nation's best crime-fighting resources. State and local police throughout the country turn to the FBI for help in their investigations.

Almost a century ago, the FBI did not exist. The bureau was established in 1908, when Attorney General Charles J. Bonaparte assembled thirty-four agents to investigate crimes against the federal government. From this small group arose the most respected and effective crime-fighting organization in the world.

The National Academy

In 1935, J. Edgar Hoover established the FBI National Academy in Quantico, Virginia, to train officers in many subjects, including leadership, law, fitness, and the latest crime-fighting techniques. Since it was opened, the academy has educated more than 35,000 agents, police officers, and other law-enforcement leaders.

Charles J. Bonaparte (1851–1921) faced the suspicion of legislators when he established the Bureau of Investigation in 1908. Many lawmakers thought Bonaparte wanted to invade the privacy of U.S. citizens.

Chapter One

The Bureau's Beginnings

When Bonaparte started the Bureau of Investigation in 1908, some members of Congress feared that he was forming a secret police force. They accused Bonaparte of wanting to spy on the nation's citizens and leaders. Despite these concerns, the bureau grew steadily over the next ten years. It investigated land fraud, bankruptcy, destruction of federal property, and murders committed on American Indian reservations.

Slackers

In 1917, the United States entered World War I. War fever swept through the country. Factories started making weapons, uniforms, tools, and tanks to equip the U.S. Army. All men of age were required to sign up for the **draft**.

Many Americans did not support the war, and many tried to avoid army service. In June 1917, Congress passed the Espionage Act, which authorized the Bureau of Investigation to pursue hundreds of thousands of men, called "slackers," who had not registered for the draft. In a series of "slacker raids," bureau agents combed through pool halls, bars, and dance halls for young men who could not produce a draft card.

At first, the public tolerated these raids—after all, the nation was fighting a war. Their tolerance came to an abrupt end in September 1918, however, when the bureau raided New York City for three days and sent more than 75,000 men to jail. These raids were heavily criticized by some leaders and journalists, who learned that only one thousand of the jailed men had been found guilty. Even worse, many of the men

No man was safe from the "slacker raids," in which Bureau of Investigation agents combed the streets of American cities for draft dodgers. Here, officials unload alleged slackers from a lumber truck in Newark, New Jersey, in 1919.

were not even of draft age. One was seventy-five years old and needed crutches to walk.

To support the slacker raids, the Bureau of Investigation relied on large numbers of civilians. Even though they were not police officers, these civilians were allowed to bully and arrest thousands of people. As public criticism of this practice became more severe, the bureau finally admitted that its actions were illegal.

The Red Scare

After World War I, the Bureau of Investigation turned its attention to a new threat: **communism**. In 1917, a communist

Steelworkers display their strike notices in Chicago, Illinois, in 1919. Labor demonstrations such as this one deepened the "red scare," a widespread fear of communist revolution in the United States.

party called the Bolsheviks violently overthrew the **czar** of Russia. Many leaders in Europe and the United States saw communism as a threat to their democratic way of life. They feared communism would spread to their own borders and topple their governments.

By 1919, it looked like that fear was becoming a reality. In that year, four million American workers went on **strike** to protest low wages. Steelworkers walked out of plants. Coal miners refused to enter their mines. In Boston, even the police stopped patrolling the streets. At the same time, violent protesters began to mail bombs to government and business leaders. In New York City, police discovered thirty bombs in mail packages. One bomb exploded on the doorstep of Attorney General A. Mitchell Palmer.

Government officials blamed communists, called "reds" because of the party's symbolic color, for the unrest. A "red scare" swept through the country. Bureau of Investigation agents kept a close watch on communist and other protest groups. They sent agents to join these organizations and to collect books, pamphlets, and newspapers. Within months, more than 200,000 groups and individuals were on file.

Throughout 1919, bureau agents and police conducted raids in over thirty cities. They arrested more than ten thousand people, most of whom were members of the Communist Party and the Communist Labor Party. Following the raids, about 550 people were forced to leave the United States. The Justice Department claimed that a revolution had been overturned.

Then troubling details came to light. The citizens arrested in the raids had been denied lawyers, and this violated their basic rights. Acting on only slight **evidence**, some bureau agents had illegally entered homes and offices in search of information.

When Louis F. Post, assistant labor secretary, learned of the bureau's tactics, he dismissed most of the cases outright. He then detailed the abuses in a speech to Congress. As a result, the excited passions of the red scare began to fade.

Scandal

In 1924, the Bureau of Investigation suffered another serious blow. Congress discovered that the attorney general had ordered bureau agents to break into two senators' offices and homes to look for embarrassing information. A storm of criticism fell on the Justice Department and the bureau. President Calvin Coolidge fired the attorney general and replaced him with Harlan F. Stone, a Columbia University law professor.

Upon taking office, Stone announced that the bureau would have no role in politics. Instead, it would be concerned

J. Edgar Hoover: A Mixed Legacy

John Edgar Hoover was born on January 1, 1895. He spent his entire life in Washington, D.C. After studying to become a lawyer, he joined the U.S. Department of Justice in 1917. In 1919, he was put in charge of the General Intelligence Division, where he monitored **radical** and communist groups. Hoover took control of the Bureau of Investigation in 1924 and held the post until his death in 1972. As director, Hoover transformed the FBI into a professional and widely respected organization. Also under his direction, however, the bureau violated the rights of thousands of Americans. Today, Hoover is remembered with a mixture of praise and criticism.

solely with enforcing the country's laws. To head the bureau, Stone promoted its assistant director, J. Edgar Hoover.

Hoover moved quickly to repair the bureau's damaged reputation. In his first year, he fired sixty-two incompetent agents and staff, scheduled inspections of field offices, and ordered reviews of each agent. He also demanded that agents wear a suit and tie at all times. "I want [my agents] to set the example in their own communities," he wrote. As Hoover labored to make the FBI more professional, a new crime wave broke across the country.

Townspeople watch as a Prohibitionist destroys a barrel of beer with an ax in the 1920s. Originally intended to rid the nation of vice and corruption, Prohibition gave rise to a new, organized kind of crime.

Chapter Two

Gangsters, Mobsters, and Spies

In 1920, Congress banned the selling and drinking of alcohol in the United States. This began the period of American history known as the Prohibition Era. In obedience to the new law, citizens split beer kegs with axes and poured the foaming liquid into gutters. They also smashed bottles of gin, vodka, and whiskey with baseball bats.

Reformers were overjoyed. Without the curse of alcohol, they thought, Americans would devote their energies to noble pursuits such as labor, art, and religion. What happened was quite different from reformers' expectations, however. When the saloons shut down, thirsty Americans simply looked for a new place to drink. The demand for alcohol surged, and prices soared.

Prohibition presented criminals with a golden opportunity. Loading alcohol into trucks and ships, they smuggled it into the United States from Canada and Mexico. They built vats in warehouses and produced millions of gallons of alcohol. Dozens of workers were needed to make, distribute, and sell alcohol. Bosses oversaw the operation by enforcing rules, tracking payments, and forcing out competitors. In the process, they made millions of dollars. Crime had become highly organized.

Organized Crime

In America's large cities, criminal gangs fought for control of the most profitable illegal businesses. With so much money at stake, the gangs often settled their disagreements with guns and knives. In 1926, the number of murders in the United States rose to above ten thousand.

Much of the new crime wave was directed by the Mafia, whose members came from Italy. Groups called families, each led by a *don*, ran all the criminal activity in an area. Although the Mafia committed many crimes, they were rarely prose-

Scarface

In the 1920s, a mobster named Al Capone led the most powerful Mafia crime gang in Chicago. Capone was a mountain of a man, with fleshy lips, a flat nose, and dark eyes. Three knife wounds that stretched across his left cheek inspired his nickname, "Scarface." As crime lord, Capone once beat two men to death with a baseball bat. In February 1929, Capone ordered his men to take seven rival gangsters into a garage and gun them down. This crime was dubbed the St. Valentine's Day Massacre.

cuted. A code of silence kept them from speaking to police, and witnesses rarely had the courage to testify in open court.

The police were overwhelmed by all this criminal activity. Many city police departments were corrupt, and criminals were therefore able to pay officers to look the other way. Town police forces were often too small and outgunned. Many gangsters perfected a technique of robbing banks and then speeding away across state lines in getaway cars.

Hoover and his bureau could do little about this crime wave. The organization was limited to pursuing crimes against the federal government. Because murder, robbery, and stealing broke state laws, it was up to town and city police forces, rather than a federal agency, to find the criminals. The resentment of police also limited the bureau's power. Local officials refused to take direction from federal agents.

The Lindbergh Case

This changed in 1932, when a horrendous crime led to an expansion of the FBI's powers. On March 1, Charles Lindbergh's twenty-month-old son was kidnapped from his home in New Jersey. Lindbergh was an extremely popular figure who had become an international hero in 1927, when he flew solo across the Atlantic Ocean.

A ransom note demanded $50,000 for the Lindbergh child's safe return. The money was given to a man who claimed that the baby was on a boat off Martha's Vineyard, Massachusetts—but the man disappeared, and the boat was never found. Six weeks later, the child's body was discovered in a grave near the Lindbergh home. He had been killed by a sharp blow to the head.

The events of the kidnapping filled the newspapers. Citizens reacted in horror, rage, and fear. If Lindbergh wasn't safe, they asked, who was?

In response, Congress passed a bill—called the Lindbergh Law—that made kidnapping a **federal crime**. In 1933, President Franklin D. Roosevelt placed the Bureau of Investigation in charge of the Lindbergh case. The break in the investigation came in September 1934, when a German immigrant, Bruno Richard Hauptmann, was spotted using one of the bills from the ransom money to pay for gas in Bronx, New York. Bureau investigators later found $14,600 of the ransom money stored in his garage.

During the trial, a bureau investigator linked Hauptmann's handwriting to the ransom note. An expert also showed that a ladder found at the crime scene came from Hauptmann's house. The bureau won its case. In April 1936, Hauptmann was convicted of murder and sentenced to death by electrocution.

Bureau investigators inspect a ladder found at the home of Charles Lindbergh in Hopewell, New Jersey, in 1932. An expert later showed that this ladder came from the house of Bruno Richard Hauptmann, who had kidnapped Lindbergh's baby son.

G-Men

In July 1933, a wealthy oilman named Charles F. Urschel was blindfolded, kidnapped, and held for a $200,000 ransom. The Bureau of Investigation took over the case. The ransom was paid, and Urschel was released safely. Urschel gave agents important clues about his captors, especially about the farmhouse where he was held. Every night and every morning, said Urschel, an airplane had flown overhead. One morning, while it rained, he had heard nothing.

Agents checked airport schedules and weather reports and discovered an airport where a plane took off every morning and landed every night. Helped by this and other tips, agents raided a farm near Paradise, Texas. The farm was owned by relatives of gangster George "Machine Gun" Kelly. The relatives confessed that Kelly was responsible for the crime.

On September 26, 1933, agents surrounded Kelly in a house in Memphis, Tennessee. When the armed agents stormed into the house, Kelly was shocked.

"Don't shoot, G-men! Don't shoot!" he stammered.

Kelly was sentenced to life imprisonment, and the legend of the G-man was born.

The word *G-men* stood for government men. In newspapers and movies, the G-man was portrayed as a national hero. Bold, confident, and well dressed, he tracked down and captured the nation's criminals.

Hoover's work was paying off. The bureau was developing a reputation for professionalism. Word spread that the G-man "always got his man." Hoover's popularity soared.

Public Enemy Number One

In the 1930s, the FBI faced criminals who carried quick-firing "Tommy" guns. One of the most famous and deadly was John Dillinger. In the spring of 1933, Dillinger and his gang went on a crime spree, robbing five Indiana and Ohio banks in less than four months. Daring, brilliant, and handsome, Dillinger caught the imagination of the public. In one famous incident, he was captured, escaped from jail, and robbed three police departments of their weapons. Newspapers eagerly reported his latest exploits. Hoover, however, was furious. He declared Dillinger "Public Enemy Number One."

Dillinger was captured in March 1934 and sent to an Illinois prison. He did not stay long, however. In his cell,

Gangster Names

The FBI pursued scores of mobsters and gangsters during the 1920s and 1930s. Many of them had colorful names, including Charles "Pretty Boy" Floyd, Lester "Baby Face" Nelson, Jack "Legs" Diamond, and Charlie "Lucky" Luciano.

Dillinger carved a piece of wood into the shape of a gun and blackened it with boot polish. The guards fell for the ruse, and Dillinger escaped in the sheriff's car.

Hoover ordered the FBI to capture Dillinger at all costs. Dillinger might have eluded the agents if not for a tip that the bureau received in July 1934. A woman said that she would be attending a movie with Dillinger at the Biograph Theater in Chicago. She told the agents that she would wear a red dress so they could spot her.

On July 22, FBI agents surrounded the theater. When Dillinger appeared, the agents ordered him to surrender. Even though he was surrounded, Dillinger reached for the pistol in his coat. The agents opened fire and killed him.

John Dillinger was so dangerous that Hoover declared him "Public Enemy Number One." Pictured here is Dillinger's wanted poster from June 1934.

WANTED

JOHN HERBERT DILLINGER

On June 23, 1934, HOMER S. CUMMINGS, Attorney General of the United States, under the authority vested in him by an Act of Congress approved June 6, 1934, offered a reward of

$10,000.00

for the capture of John Herbert Dillinger or a reward of

$5,000.00

for information leading to the arrest of John Herbert Dillinger.

DESCRIPTION

Age, 32 years; Height, 5 feet 7-1/8 inches; Weight, 153 pounds; Build, medium; Hair, medium chestnut; Eyes, grey; Complexion, medium; Occupation, machinist; Marks and scars, 1/2 inch scar back left hand, scar middle upper lip, brown mole between eyebrows.

All claims to any of the aforesaid rewards and all questions and disputes that may arise as among claimants to the foregoing rewards shall be passed upon by the Attorney General and his decisions shall be final and conclusive. The right is reserved to divide and allocate portions of any of said rewards as between several claimants. No part of the aforesaid rewards shall be paid to any official or employee of the Department of Justice.

If you are in possession of any information concerning the whereabouts of John Herbert Dillinger, communicate immediately by telephone or telegraph collect to the nearest office of the Division of Investigation, United States Department of Justice, the local addresses of which are set forth on the reverse side of this notice.

Nazis and Communists

In 1933, the Prohibition amendment was **repealed**, and it appeared that the crime wave was finally coming to an end. Then a new threat appeared from Europe. In the 1930s, both Germany and Italy had fallen under the rule of **dictators**. German leader Adolf Hitler plotted to dominate the world with his Nazi Party. President Roosevelt told Hoover to watch Nazi groups closely, and the FBI switched from chasing gangsters to catching spies.

In December 1941, the United States entered World War II against Germany, Italy, and Japan. To cripple the American war effort, the Germans sent agents to the United States to blow up factories and railroad bridges. In June 1942, the FBI arrested seven German agents who had landed in Long Island and Florida. Five of the spies were sentenced to death one month later. The other two, including their leader, George John Dasch, were given lighter sentences for turning in their compatriots.

After the war ended, the FBI led the investigation of spies during the **Cold War**, a time of great tension

Surrounded by fellow Nazis, Hitler delivers a speech in Berlin, Germany, in 1937. The FBI worked hard to fight Nazi spies throughout the 1930s and 1940s.

Ten Most Wanted Fugitives

In 1950, the FBI began releasing the Ten Most Wanted, a list of names and descriptions of the most dangerous criminals in the United States. The bureau put the list on posters and hung them in post offices and other public buildings. Since the Ten Most Wanted was first posted, 458 criminals have made the list, and 429 have been captured. The list is still posted today.

between the former Soviet Union and the United States. When the Soviet Union detonated its first atomic bomb in 1949, Hoover immediately suspected that a spy had stolen the plans for the American bomb that had been detonated in 1945. He dubbed this the "crime of the century."

FBI agents followed a trail of spies that led to a man named

Julius Rosenberg, whose spy ring had stolen the secrets of the American atom bomb. Agents arrested Julius and his wife, Ethel, in July 1950. They were found guilty on March 29, 1951, and later were put to death. Today, many people question whether the Rosenbergs were guilty of the crime of the century.

Ethel and Julius Rosenberg sit in a police van soon after being declared guilty of espionage, April 1951, New York City.

When the civil-rights movement began in the 1950s, the FBI did very little to address the violence that sprang up at demonstrations throughout the South. Soon the bureau could no longer ignore it. Here, two boys declare their pride at a protest march in the 1960s.

I AM
A
MAN

I AM
A

Chapter Three

Protests and Assassinations

In the 1950s and 1960s, African-Americans raised their voices in protest against their unequal status in American society. Black students were separated from white students, and they attended crumbling schools. They could not get important jobs in the government, at banks, or in universities. Laws required that they drink from separate water fountains, swim in separate pools, and sit at the back of buses.

The protests started in the South. Under the leadership of Martin Luther King, Jr., African-Americans organized and marched to make their cause heard. Protesters often faced angry crowds and hostile police officers. These confrontations led to beatings, bloodshed, and sometimes murder.

Many civil-rights leaders looked to the FBI for protection because local police often did nothing to stop the violence. At first, Hoover distrusted the marchers. He disliked protest, and he suspected that the movement was funded and directed by communists. Thus, during the early 1960s, the FBI did little to help the civil-rights movement.

Then, during the summer of 1964, black and white students traveled into the South to protest racism. On June 21, three young civil-rights workers were murdered and buried in an earth dam. A national outcry followed, and more than 250 FBI agents investigated the case. After several months, the FBI arrested nineteen members of the **Ku Klux Klan**, a white-supremacist organization, for the murders. Seven people were eventually sentenced to jail. To increase the presence of the FBI in the South, Hoover opened a field office in Jackson, Mississippi, on July 10, 1964.

Fallen Leaders

On November 22, 1963, President John F. Kennedy, beginning his campaign for reelection in 1964, was riding in an open limousine in Dallas, Texas. As the car passed the city's book-depository building, a sniper fired three shots at the motorcade. The third shot hit Kennedy in the back of the head. He died later that day at Parkland Memorial Hospital.

The nation, mourning the loss of their president, demanded a full investigation of the assassination. The new president, Lyndon B. Johnson, turned to the FBI for answers. Agents combed through the crime scene, conducted more than 25,000 interviews, and wrote 2,300 reports. Based on the FBI investigation, a special government commission called the Warren Commission concluded that the gunman, Lee Harvey Oswald, had acted alone.

Investigators reenact President John F. Kennedy's 1963 assassination in Dallas, Texas, about six months after the event. In the foreground, agents use cameras to document different perspectives and angles.

Just as the nation was recovering from Kennedy's death, two more of its leaders fell to assassins' bullets. On April 4, 1968, civil-rights leader Martin Luther King, Jr., was shot and killed in Memphis, Tennessee. Soon after, in June 1968, Robert F. Kennedy, John's brother and now a candidate for the presidency, was shot and killed. Thousands of FBI agents investigated both of these cases. They tracked down leads, interviewed witnesses, and helped bring the killers—James Earl Ray and Sirhan B. Sirhan—to justice.

COINTELPRO

In 1965, American soldiers were sent to fight in the Asian nation of South Vietnam. Many Americans, especially young people on college campuses, protested the war as unjust. As

A professor at Columbia University finds an entrance blocked by students during a sit-in protesting the Vietnam War in April 1968. This and other demonstrations led to COINTELPRO, an FBI operation in which agents secretly—and illegally—investigated radical groups.

the number of war casualties grew, so did the protests. Groups formed to criticize the government and its policies.

Hoover was convinced that these groups were simply dedicated to breaking the law. He ordered the FBI to watch them closely and to disrupt them whenever possible. The FBI's operations were called COINTELPRO, which is short for counterintelligence program.

The FBI used many different tactics in COINTELPRO. One of these tactics involved **informants** who joined the groups and reported back to the bureau, which then attempted to divide the groups' leadership. Hoover secretly investigated many groups, including the Ku Klux Klan, militant African-American groups, and communist organizations. Between 1958 and 1971, the FBI conducted more than 2,300 COINTELPRO operations.

In the Wake of Hoover

On May 2, 1972, J. Edgar Hoover died. President Richard Nixon ordered that his body lie in state in the Capitol building, an honor given to only twenty-two other Americans up to that time. Hoover received that honor because he had made the FBI a professional, efficient, and respected force. He also had been responsible for many of its abuses of power, however. In the years following Hoover's death, the reputation of the FBI would sink to the lowest point in its history.

The bureau's loss of prestige began a year before Hoover's death. On March 8, 1971, burglars broke into an FBI office in

Media, Pennsylvania. When investigators arrived the next morning, they found that hundreds of secret COINTELPRO documents had been stolen. The group behind the burglary thought the FBI had too much power. To expose the bureau's abuses, they sent the documents to government leaders and to the press. Many of the documents, which revealed the existence of COINTELPRO, were published in the *New York Times* and the *Washington Post*.

FBI leaders defended COINTELPRO as necessary to protect the nation during dangerous times. Many in the public and the press disagreed, however. To them, the FBI was a corrupt government agency that snooped on its citizens and harassed them for their beliefs.

In 1973, the new FBI director, William D. Ruckelshaus, admitted that the bureau had planted seventeen **wiretaps** between 1969 and 1973. The phones tapped included those of government employees and news reporters. In 1975, the country learned that Hoover had kept secret files filled with embarrassing information on public figures in the United States.

Congress took a close look at FBI techniques, especially "black-bag jobs," in which agents illegally broke into buildings to find information. In 1975, the Socialist Workers Party sued the FBI for $27 million for violating its constitutional rights. Bureau records later revealed that the FBI had broken into the party's headquarters ninety-three times. The heroic myth of the G-man was shattered.

FBI director William Ruckelshaus admits that the FBI tapped the phones of government employees and reporters during the COINTELPRO operations. This photograph was taken on May 14, 1973, in Washington, D.C.

Since the 1970s, the FBI has kept its focus on the nation's most damaging criminals. Here, an agent escorts mobster Gariat Iousoupbekov from a building in New York City on July 9, 1998.

Chapter Four

Reform

After the scandals of the early 1970s, the FBI stopped investigating smaller, less important criminal cases. Instead, it took a "quality over quantity" approach that continues to this day. The bureau concentrated its resources on the criminals who did the most damage—drug smugglers, terrorists, spies, serial murderers, organized crime bosses, and **white-collar criminals**. The FBI also worked to make its staff more diverse.

Crimes Without Weapons

Not all criminals use guns and bombs. Some of them are known as white-collar criminals—professionals who abuse their positions of power. A white-collar criminal might be a doctor who bills the government for an operation that he never performed. Another might be a builder who uses faulty material in construction but charges the full price anyway.

Politicians who break the law are also considered white-collar criminals. In the late 1970s, FBI agents posed as wealthy Arabs and approached government officials in a secret operation. The disguised agents offered the officials large sums of money in exchange for political favors. One Congressman, Michael Myers, took $50,000 to help an Arab citizen get protection in the United States. Eventually, seven Congressmen were convicted of accepting bribes.

The Year of the Spy

Along with protecting the United States from crime, the FBI protects the nation's secrets. During the Cold War, FBI agents constantly monitored the actions of Soviet diplomats in Washington, D.C. They also looked out for Americans who might pass on the nation's secrets to the Soviets. In 1985, a woman named Barbara Walker contacted the FBI. She reported that her husband had dropped packages in the woods and had returned with cash. It appeared that he was passing secret documents on to the Soviets.

The FBI watched John A. Walker, Jr., closely and tapped his phone. For six weeks, agents saw and heard nothing unusual. Then, in May 1985, Walker left his house in his car.

The Winning Cheeseburger

In August 2001, the FBI arrested a white-collar criminal who had rigged a contest at a popular fast-food restaurant chain. He had stolen prize pieces and given them to his friends.

He drove strangely, often stopping suddenly and turning around as if to throw followers off his trail. FBI agents in cars lost sight of him, but an FBI airplane followed his route from overhead.

Barbara Walker, it turned out, was right about her husband. A Soviet man had left soda-pop cans along the road to show Walker where to drop the documents and collect his money. Later, agents arrested Walker in his hotel room. They learned that Walker had sold the Soviets valuable information, including ship plans, base locations, and secret codes. He was sentenced to life in prison. Walker was the FBI's first success in what became known as the "year of the spy."

A More Diverse FBI

For most of its history, the FBI hired only white males as agents. In 1972, fewer than 200 agents—out of 8,659— were African-American, Latino, Asian, or American Indian. None were women.

In 1978, FBI director William Webster began recruiting female and

After pleading guilty to spying for the former Soviet Union, John A. Walker, Jr., is escorted to the federal court in Baltimore, Maryland, in October 1985. The FBI was central to bringing Walker to justice in what became known as the "year of the spy."

Hogan's Alley

In Hogan's Alley, FBI agents arrest criminals every day. Hogan's Alley is a fake town—complete with a bank, a post office, and a drug store—at the FBI Academy. In Hogan's Alley, agents learn to operate guns and to make arrests. The criminals are played by actors.

minority agents. When Webster left the bureau in 1987, the number of minority agents had increased from 413 to 943. The number of female agents had jumped to 787.

Minority and female FBI agents have not always felt welcome in the bureau, however, and many have battled **discrimination**. In a lawsuit in the early 1980s, about three hundred Latino agents claimed that they were denied high-profile assignments and top positions because of their ethnic background. In 1988, a federal judge agreed. As a result, eleven

Latino agents were given new positions and higher salaries.

In 1992, the FBI faced a similar lawsuit, this time from African-American agents who felt they had been treated unfairly. FBI director William S. Sessions agreed to change things. He promoted six African-American agents and assigned another nine to headquarters in Washington, D.C.

In 1993, female FBI agents also spoke out against discrimination. In response, Director Louis Freeh promised to make the bureau more diverse. He promoted the first Latino, the first woman, and two additional African-Americans to high-level positions in the FBI. Today, of more than 11,000 total FBI agents, 1,400 are of minority backgrounds, and another 1,500 are women.

Throughout the 1990s, FBI directors worked to make the bureau more diverse. Here, two female agents check their progress at target practice.

Theodore Kaczynski, also known as the Unabomber, represented a new threat to the FBI: terrorism from within U.S. borders.

Chapter Five

New Challenges

In the 1990s and into the twenty-first century, the FBI faced new challenges. The Cold War had ended, and Director Sessions reassigned hundreds of agents from catching spies to catching criminals. The FBI also had to investigate several **terrorists**—people who use actions of terror, such as bombing and hijacking, to advance their cause.

Bombers

In the mid-1990s, FBI agents uncovered a serious plot to blow up New York City

45

landmarks such as the United Nations building and the Holland and Lincoln Tunnels. Twelve people either plead guilty or were found guilty of the crime. Discovering this plot was a major accomplishment for the FBI.

In 1996, agents tracked down and arrested Theodore J. Kaczynski—the man known as the Unabomber—with help from Kaczynski's brother. Since 1978, Kaczynski had sent or planted sixteen bombs throughout the United States. Most of the bombs failed to do any damage, but others were deadly: three people died, and another twenty-three were wounded.

Bloodshed at Ruby Ridge

In August 1992, U.S. marshals approached an isolated mountain cabin in Ruby Ridge, Idaho. Inside the cabin lived Randall Weaver and his family. The marshals considered Weaver a dangerous fugitive; about a year before, he had illegally sold two shotguns to a federal agent.

On August 21, Weaver and the marshals stumbled into each other in the thick forest around the cabin. Both sides pulled their guns and began firing. In the exchange, Weaver's fourteen-year-old son, Samuel, and Marshall William Degan were killed.

The marshals then called in the FBI, whose Hostage Rescue Team showed up the next day and surrounded the cabin. FBI snipers were given orders that allowed them to shoot any adult near the cabin.

On August 22, a sniper, thinking Weaver was about to

Randall Weaver displays the bullet-ridden door of his Ruby Ridge, Idaho, cabin as he testifies before a Senate judiciary subcommittee in Washington, D.C., in September 1995. The FBI was severely criticized for how it handled the bloody 1992 shootout, in which Weaver's wife and son were killed.

shoot at a helicopter hovering overhead, aimed and fired, wounding Weaver. Weaver and a friend ran back to the cabin. The sniper fired again, and this time he hit Weaver's friend, Kevin Harris. Another of the sniper's bullets punched through the cabin door and hit Weaver's wife, Vicki. The sniper had not seen her there. Vicki later died from her wounds.

After ten more days, Weaver surrendered. The bloody siege at Ruby Ridge raised disturbing questions, however. Had the FBI used too much force? Was the sniper wrong in firing the shots? Why did three people—one of them a teenager—have to die during the capture?

Ruby Ridge turned public reaction against the FBI. A jury refused to convict Weaver for the murder of Degan. Later, the FBI conducted its own investigation of Ruby Ridge. In 1995 and 1997, FBI director Louis Freeh took disciplinary action against agents and their directors for the bloody events.

Flames at Waco

In February 1993, agents from the Bureau of Alcohol, Tobacco, and Firearms approached a compound outside Waco, Texas. Inside lived more than one hundred Branch Davidians, members of a religious group led by a man named David Koresh, who had illegally stockpiled guns and ammunition in the compound. In a bloody gun battle, four agents and six Branch Davidians were killed. The FBI was called in.

For the next fifty-one days, FBI agents urged the Branch Davidians to surrender, but Koresh released only thirty-five people from the compound. About eighty-five others, including twenty-five children under the age of fifteen, remained inside. In April, the new attorney general, Janet Reno, approved an attack on the compound. The FBI planned to slowly inject tear gas into the buildings. When the air became impossible to breathe, agents thought, the Davidians would be forced to abandon the compound peacefully.

When the FBI tank started pumping in tear gas, however, the Davidians did not flee. As agents and observers watched in horror, several fires appeared in the building. Fanned by winds, a giant blaze consumed the structure within minutes. Koresh, the twenty-five children, and about fifty followers died.

The FBI was angrily criticized in Congress and in the media. Some said that the bureau should have used different tactics to end the standoff. Others blamed the catastrophe on Koresh. Some radical groups, angered by the Waco disaster, vowed to take revenge on the U.S. government.

Disaster at Oklahoma City

Two years after the Waco raid, on April 19, 1995, a rental truck pulled up in front of the Alfred P. Murrah Federal Building in Oklahoma City. Shortly after 9 A.M., a massive homemade bomb in the truck's cargo bay detonated. The explosion tore into the nine-story structure, smashing windows, crushing floors, and eating a giant hole in the building. More than 165 government workers and bystanders were

FBI investigators survey the rubble of the Branch Davidians' compound in Waco, Texas, after the building's inhabitants set it on fire in 1993.

FBI and other emergency workers stand at the foot of the ruined Alfred P. Murrah Federal Building in Oklahoma City during a memorial service honoring the 168 people killed in the April 19, 1995, bombing.

killed, including 15 children in the day-care center. Another 850 people were wounded.

FBI and other government agents began investigating the case immediately. Within hours, the truck's axle was found a block away from the explosion. Agents traced the identification number to a body shop in Junction City, Kansas. From

there, the agents traced the bomber's hotel room. The bomber had registered with his real name: Timothy McVeigh.

The FBI conducted 25,000 interviews in connection with the bombing and collected 7,000 pounds (3,200 kilograms) of evidence for McVeigh's trial. In June 1997, McVeigh was convicted and sentenced to death. Terry Nichols, a friend and helper to McVeigh, was sentenced to life imprisonment.

The FBI was proud of its role in convicting McVeigh, but the case also proved to be a major embarrassment to the bureau. Weeks before McVeigh's scheduled execution, his lawyers learned that the FBI had neglected to turn over more

State and federal agents lead Timothy McVeigh, second from the left, from an Oklahoma courthouse in April 1995.

than four thousand case documents. Despite the blunder, McVeigh was executed in 2001.

Into the Twenty-first Century

The founders of the FBI probably would not recognize it today. The bureau has grown from a tiny organization with limited powers to a giant, well-funded, respected police force. Its crime-fighting techniques are studied and copied around the world.

As the FBI enters the twenty-first century, it continues to face new challenges. The September 11, 2001, terrorist attacks did more than change the nation; they also dramatically changed the FBI and its mission. One month after the attacks, President Bush and his advisors announced a plan to refocus the FBI on counterterrorism. Thousands of agents were told to drop their cases and to focus on preventing more terrorist attacks on American soil. The days of solely arresting bank robbers and busting drug rings were over. A new, more sophisticated criminal had appeared.

Timeline

1908	U.S. Attorney General Charles J. Bonaparte creates the Bureau of Investigation under the Department of Justice.
1917	Congress passes the Espionage Act.
1919–1920	In reaction to the "red scare," bureau agents arrest hundreds of communists.
1924	J. Edgar Hoover is appointed director on May 10.
1932	The Bureau of Investigation's crime laboratory is established.
1933	Bureau agents capture George "Machine Gun" Kelly on June 23. The bureau takes charge of the Lindbergh kidnapping investigation.
1935	The Bureau of Investigation is renamed the Federal Bureau of Investigation (FBI) on July 1. The FBI National Academy is started on July 29.
1950	On March 14, the FBI posts its Ten Most Wanted Fugitives list for the first time.
1958	Hoover authorizes the first COINTELPRO operation.
1963	President John F. Kennedy is assassinated in Dallas on November 22, launching one of the biggest investigations in FBI history.
1964	Three civil-rights workers are murdered near Philadelphia, Mississippi, on June 21.

continued on next page

Timeline *(continued)*

1968	Martin Luther King, Jr., is assassinated in Memphis, Tennessee, on April 5.
1972	J. Edgar Hoover dies on May 2.
1985	John A. Walker, Jr., is arrested by the FBI on May 1.
1992	Three people die in a confrontation between FBI agents and Randall Weaver in Ruby Ridge, Idaho.
1993	Fires lead to the death of more than seventy-five Branch Davidians in Waco, Texas.
1995	On April 19, a bomb is detonated at the Alfred P. Murrah Federal Building in Oklahoma City, and 168 people die.
2001	In February, Robert Hanssen, a top FBI agent, is charged with spying for the Russians. On September 11, terrorists hijack four planes and fly them into the World Trade Center, the Pentagon, and a field in Pennsylvania.
February– March 2002	A record fifteen thousand Americans apply for special agent positions in the FBI. This is partly in response to the September 2001 terrorist attacks.

Glossary

agent—an FBI worker who investigates crimes and makes arrests

Cold War—a period of hostility between the United States and the former Soviet Union that lasted from 1945 to 1991. The war was said to be cold because the two countries never fought directly with each other.

communism—a political system in which all property is centralized and shared

czar—the name for the ruler of Russia before the 1917 revolution

dictator—a person who rules a country with complete and total power

discrimination—unfair treatment of a person because of his or her race, gender, sexual orientation, or religious beliefs

draft—the recruitment of people for required military service

evidence—materials used to prove a crime

federal crime—a crime that can be prosecuted by federal agents, as opposed to a state crime, which is prosecuted by local police forces

fidelity—loyalty; faithfulness

informant—a person who joins a group and then reveals its workings to outsiders

integrity—honesty; uprightness

Ku Klux Klan—an American hate group that supports the separation of white and black people

radical—a person who advocates extreme changes in an existing political or social system

repeal—to take back; to retract

strike—a refusal to work in order to bargain for higher pay or benefits

terrorist—a person who seeks to advance his or her cause through secretive, violent activities

white-collar criminals—people who commit nonviolent crimes, such as fraud, tax evasion, and bribery, by abusing their positions of power

wiretap—an electronic device that allows someone to record another person's words

To Find Out More

Books

Balcavage, Dynise. Arthur Schlesinger (ed.). *The Federal Bureau of Investigation*. Philadelphia: Chelsea House Publishers, 2000.

Italia, Robert. *Courageous Crimefighters*. Minneapolis: Oliver Press, 1995.

Meltzer, Milton. *Case Closed: The Real Scoop on Detective Work*. New York: Scholastic, 2001.

Trespacz, Karen L. *The Trial of Gangster Al Capone: A Headline Court Case*. Springfield, NJ: Enslow Publishing, 2001.

Videos

G-Men: The Rise of J. Edgar Hoover, PBS, 1981.

J. Edgar Hoover: Private and Confidential, A & E Network, 1999.

Al Capone: Scarface, A & E Home Video, 1996.

Organization and Online Site

www.fbi.gov
http://www.fbi.gov/kids/6th12th/6th12th.htm
The homepage of the Federal Bureau of Investigation provides a wealth of information on the FBI, including an FBI "field trip" for students.

A Note on Sources

To research this book, I read several books and articles, both in magazines and online. I found several to be particularly helpful. The recently published *The FBI: A Comprehensive Reference Guide*, edited by Athan G. Theoharis, gives an excellent overview of the bureau and its history, controversies, and culture. I found Ronald Kessler's *The FBI* to be a wonderful source on the modern FBI. Kessler's other book, *Spy vs. Spy*, tells the fascinating story of the FBI's counterintelligence program. The FBI headquarters in Washington, D.C., which is open to tours, provides an intimate look at artifacts of the FBI and how the bureau works today.

—*Brendan January*

Index

Numbers in *italics* indicate illustrations.

About the Author

Brendan January is an award-winning author of more than twenty nonfiction books for young readers. He is a graduate of Haverford College, Pennsylvania, and Columbia Graduate School of Journalism. January is currently a journalist at the *Philadelphia Inquirer* and lives with his wife in Jersey City.